VOICE OF THE SOULS

ORACLE

T0405398

VOICE OF THE SOULS
ORACLE

ISABELLE CERF
Illustrations by Daphna Sebbane

ROCKPOOL

A Rockpool book
PO Box 252
Summer Hill
NSW 2130
Australia

rockpoolpublishing.com
Follow us! **f** **⊙** rockpoolpublishing
Tag your images with #rockpoolpublishing

First published as *L'oracle de la Voix des Âmes* under
ISBN 9782361883980, by Éditions Exergue,
a trademark of Guy Trédaniel publishing group.

This edition published in 2022 by Rockpool Publishing

ISBN: 9781922579423

Design and typesetting by Daniel Poole, Rockpool Publishing
Original text translated by Geraldine de Vries
English text edited by Jess Cox

Printed and bound in China

10 9 8 7 6 5 4 3

Hi friend,

When we talk about psychic ability, we sometimes call it a 'gift'. At times, we also believe it's dangerous or frightening, or that it doesn't exist at all. While I can't say if this is right or wrong, it doesn't resonate with my frame of reference.

Psychic ability is being able to contact souls on the other side and/or with one's spirit guides. It's a natural connection to your third-eye and crown chakras. Your psychic ability's power depends on your past lives, your open-mindedness, and the balance of your chakras. To develop your psychic ability, trust in your feelings. If you are scared or motivated by controlling or spiritually egotistic energies, you'll find it difficult to connect to this capability.

Psychic ability is not refusing to mourn. It's not here to reassure us, nor help us flee or control an unbearable situation or loss. Mourning occurs in stages and is experienced at one's own pace. If you are in the process of mourning, I send you much love and comfort, and I invite you to experience this time with love and compassion.

Another limiting belief is that you are controlled by your own psychic ability, which may produce frightening experiences. This is not true. We are all psychic on different levels, and it is our unconscious choice to be dominated by it or not. Everyone has their own reasons, but if you feel you're subject to your psychic ability, think about the secondary benefit of this feeling – it reassures a part of you.

Every psychic ability is different, and there are various channels and methods to connect to it. I don't believe in rules and rituals that work for everyone, because we all have our own resonance. Here is some advice to help you explore your psychic ability.

1. GROUND YOURSELF

To connect to your psychic ability, ground yourself; this will give you a strong connection with Earth and a positive experience of connecting to your ability. You can do this through a mindfulness meditation or guided meditation, or by going for a walk, doing a physical activity, working with a grounding stone and so on.. Find the method that works best for you.

2. BE IN A HEALTHY AND SERENE PLACE

When you connect to your psychic ability, your room is important and will need a high frequency level.

Check this either by using a pendulum or trusting in your feelings when you're there. Don't practise your psychic ability if you're feeling sad or angry. You may get no results, or be disappointed in those you do. Don't try to control things, and don't have any expectations.

To practise your psychic ability, your energy needs to be that of letting go and wellbeing. Be in the present moment without any expectations, and be open to receiving messages.

3. PSYCHIC ABILITY IS AN ENCOUNTER

It's an encounter between two souls. Having an intense experience doesn't necessarily mean that the experience will be the same each time. Each encounter is a unique moment with a particular intensity, duration and connection.

4. PAY ATTENTION TO YOUR FEELINGS

Your psychic ability may express itself through flashes, emotions, physical sensations, words you hear, or scenes or faces you see.

5. PERSEVERE

The more you develop your psychic ability, the more you'll find yourself in tune with your spiritual capabilities. Take time to discover and experience your psychic ability.

I wish you a beautiful spiritual experience and beautiful encounters.

Love, Isa

CONTENTS

SOUL CONNECTION CARDS' MESSAGES ... 105

ABOUT THE AUTHOR 117

ABOUT THE ILLUSTRATOR...........................118

OWNING YOUR ORACLE

This oracle is a tool to help you develop your capabilities. Ultimately, I hope you'll create your own reading method, with each card embodying your feelings. Along the way you'll gradually free yourself from the booklet and connect to your own psychic ability.

This oracle aims to help you encounter three different souls:

1. YOUR OWN SOUL

Sometimes, we're so busy responding to others in our daily lives, we no longer pay attention to ourselves. We may feel disconnected and find ourselves doing or experiencing things that no longer hold meaning for us. We're no longer in tune with our souls. With this oracle, you can reconnect with your own self.

2. YOUR SPIRIT GUIDES

Your spirit guides are here to help, support and protect you. They're not your servants and won't bring you everything you want. Sometimes, your wants may be different from your needs. You may feel like you don't see or understand the signs they send your way. This oracle will help you to connect with your spirit guides.

3. OTHER SOULS

Your psychic ability helps you to connect with souls on the other side. Also called 'entities', these souls may be directly connected to you, perhaps through ties in this life or from a previous existence. They may be connected to a place, object or another person. They may also be complete strangers to you. These entities may need to communicate a message or you may wish to request or pass on information to them. This oracle will support your connection with these souls.

HOW TO USE
THE CARDS

To prepare for a session with this oracle, sit in a calm and serene spot. If you like, meditate before getting started. Decide with whom you wish to communicate – with yourself, your spirit guides or an entity. Pay attention to your feelings. If you feel negative energy or emotions, or if you're having negative thoughts, take time to understand why. Work on your energy, and take up your reading again when your energy is completely positive.

Begin by closing your eyes and shuffling the cards. Cut the deck in half, then look at the two cards revealed by the cut. These two messages represent the energy of the reading. Let the feeling and message of the reading come to you.

Replace the two halves of the deck. Spread out the cards before you and select three cards. If you feel you need only one card, or more than three, follow that feeling. To clarify the message you're receiving, you can draw an additional card and place it over one of the cards already selected. Beyond the cards' messages, pay attention to your feelings. Write down what comes to you.

You can do a three-card spread connected to a single soul.

ONE SOUL

Alternatively, you can read the three cards in connection to three different souls. Here, the first card represents a message from your own soul, the second a message from your spirit guides, and the third a message from the entity you have decided to communicate with.

YOUR SOUL   **SPIRIT GUIDES**   **THE ENTITY**

If you feel the messages don't make sense, or you don't feel anything, take time to understand why. Pay attention to these energies. Attend to your self-care, and reschedule your reading for later.

THE SOUL CONNECTION CARDS

In this oracle, there are 10 soul connection cards, each holding a special energy. These cards aim to help you free yourself from the interpretations provided by this booklet, and give you confidence in your psychic ability. When getting started on your first readings, you can either remove these cards from the deck, leave them in the deck and connect with them, or work on your psychic ability using only these cards.

When you draw a soul connection card, take a deep breath and look at the illustration. Let everything you feel come to you. Look at the card as long as you need to, and write down all your feelings.

THE CARDS'
MESSAGES

ABUNDANCE

YOUR SOUL

You can have everything you need but, please, listen to me. A part of your energy is flowing too quickly and, because of this, you may feel we aren't connected. You may be moving forward too quickly, not taking the time to integrate all the signs and synchronicities you receive. Nothing happens without reason; each event and encounter has something to teach you. If you don't take the time to experience and understand them, you may feel like you're standing still

Know that abundance is there and accessible for you. To connect with me, take time to breathe and free your solar plexus chakra. Make time for meditation and deep breathing. You'll realise you can move forward with greater inner calm and serenity, and you'll look at everything happening around you with fresh eyes. You'll ground yourself through breathing, and free yourself from the energy of stagnation.

Everything will take on a new meaning.

YOUR SPIRIT GUIDES

We invite you to move forward in stages. You may wish to avoid some of these stages, thinking you don't need them. Yet, they're important for you to create new, stable and durable foundations. Some things you don't know yet, and by fully experiencing these stages, you'll find yourself in a new energy of discovering yourself and others, and the meaning of events around you.

Decide on your priorities and the time you wish to spend on them, then determine the practical goals you wish to achieve. This logic may frighten you, but it's necessary for you to be in a grounding energy. You'll keep your natural and spontaneous character, while channelling your energies to focus on yourself and your expectations.

Move forward with sure steps and with respect for your chosen path, so you may be in an energy of abundance.

THE ENTITY

I had long searched for abundance, but I now realise I was looking in the wrong places. I had not really understood this notion. I thought abundance was only material, but it is so much more than that.

Perhaps, I had shut myself away in an armour of energy, and didn't pay attention to my needs.

Material wealth contributes to happiness, but does not create it. Only you can bring happiness to yourself. Material wealth brings stability so you can pay attention to yourself. Don't be afraid of not having enough. When you're connected to yourself, abundance is already there. Material abundance is a reflection of everything you bring into yourself.

I am here to help you be in an energy of abundance. Pay attention to signs regarding material and financial issues; I will guide you towards that fulfilment, so you may have everything you need and discover new things in yourself. There are many wonders still to discover.

HELP

YOUR SOUL

You feel unable to do things correctly. At this moment, you feel alone. Everything feels complicated, and you feel only you can manage others. You feel others are abandoning you, one after the other, leaving you to face all these obligations alone.

But you're not alone, because I'm here. I am and will always be at your side. Take some time to connect with me. Sometimes, you may feel things are blocked. As if something were blocked inside you. That is me, inviting you to take a break to hear my wise counsel.

For now, take a few minutes of silence in your day. A few minutes of rest. This will help you hear me. Know that you have all the capabilities you need to take up the challenges you are facing. They are not insurmountable.

I am with you and, together, we will move forward in a positive way.

YOUR SPIRIT GUIDES

We are sending you signs to help you become aware that you can move forward alone. You feel you can't accomplish important things on your own. Yet you have a great capability to adapt, and you can show great perseverance.

We are sending you many signs related to the number 18. Remember what happened when you turned 18, and what happened 18 months ago. You experienced important things at those times, which enabled you to forge great inner resilience.

You are capable of great things, but we wish you to also remember everything you have already accomplished. You feel we are not with you, but we are always at your side. For a few months, try acting on your own and become aware of your inner strength.

We are here, but we don't act, because it's up to you to build your own path and create your own positive evolution. That is the goal of your incarnation.

THE ENTITY

I know you're asking for my help. I know that when you think of me, your throat immediately tightens. I know you feel I could help you more. But that is not my role.

I used to find it difficult to accept help from others. I thought it wasn't right for me, and I was also afraid of being criticised later on. And so, I did many things alone. That put me through difficult experiences, but it was instructive for my soul.

I am with you, but my role is not to help you directly. I am here to bring you joy so you may awaken your inner child. I put things on your path that can make you smile and bring you lightness. I am here so you may take a breather and just be in the moment.

LOVE

YOUR SOUL

I have only one message for you today, but it is an important one: 'Love yourself.'

Do not try to find love in others; do not look for a mirror in which to see yourself. You are creating emotional dependence, and you are running away from your own love. By loving yourself, you can create healthy relationships and situations in your outer life.

Your soul is wonderful but, as an incarnated being, you are imperfect. As are all the people around you. You have had experiences that you view as mistakes just like everyone else. You have been clumsy, just like

14

everyone else. You have felt that you were taking a wrong path, just like everyone else.

Love yourself, in that complete imperfection and clumsiness. Your soul is perfect and, by experiencing the imperfection, you connect to the energy of wisdom.

YOUR SPIRIT GUIDES

The energy of love will open the door to a renewal for you within the next three months.

You have long been caught in repeating patterns. You have long been caught in emotional fatigue, which guided you and projected a negative image of yourself back to you. You have released many old beliefs and thoughts. What you are missing now is true love for yourself, the compassion with which you know how to look upon others but not yourself.

Look upon yourself with love. Respect your convictions and values. Accept your dark side without looking to fight it.

Within the next three months, a wave of love will come into your outer life. It will be an echo of the love you're building for yourself. Love yourself, love life, love your past, love your experiences, love what is obvious, love synchronicities.

THE ENTITY

Remember this from me: for always and forever, I love you.

My love for you has always been strong, even if I haven't always managed to express it. I know you have expected more proof of my love. I know I could have done more, told you more that I love you, made you feel it more. That love is unbroken today. I expect nothing in return.

My energy is of unconditional love. Feel it so you may forge a new relationship with yourself. So you may move forward gently and benevolently. Feel my presence at night when you go to bed, or when you're in your car, or when you are sitting quietly. I am by your side.

Remember the rose. I manifest myself using this as a sign. The rose is my support, my presence, and your guide to help you connect to the beauty of your soul. Remember this energy of love that is your essence.

LEARNING

YOUR SOUL

You are learning many things at the moment that may not be positive. You are in an energy of intense learning and great positive evolution. You need to learn new things. You also have many abilities and skills dormant inside you. This is powerful in you.

I know you are in doubt right now. You may wonder if you're taking the right path by learning new things or making important changes related to your new capabilities. If you make the choice by and for yourself, it will always be a good choice, because it is your own. Be daring, and be confident in yourself.

I am sending you many signs to help you trust what you feel deep inside, instead of listening to other people's frameworks of reference. You are taking a unique path that will be fabulous and bring you many new things.

It will be more than sublime.

YOUR SPIRIT GUIDES

Four years ago, you experienced something important. Something you may have put on hold or kept dormant in your energies.

We are sending you many signs today because there is something important to be learned in connection to that past experience. We are sending you signs in your dreams. We advise you to write them down. If you don't remember them, take time to meditate for a few moments before going to bed, setting the intention of remembering your dreams afterwards.

You may feel caught in repetitive patterns, but that is not the only feeling coming to you. You are in an energy of new things and important changes. The next four months will be rich in events which will ask you to trust in the unknown. Trust in synchronicities.

Everything will be more than fine.

THE ENTITY

My past life taught me many things. I often talked negatively, and sometimes, I felt that life was really tough. I can still see myself ranting, or feeling everything was against me. Today, I understand these experiences were to teach me important lessons. I also understand that my soul chose this. While things felt difficult in the moment, today, I am in a positive evolution.

In my past life, I always felt tired, which prevented me from doing important things. Today, I realise I was experiencing inner duality, I was refusing to trust in life. I have no regrets. Everything I experienced was because of choices, but I will definitely do things differently in my next life.

Be yourself in this energy of learning. I will manifest myself to you through the number 13. It will be a sign of my presence that I am by your side in the new wonderment being created for you. Have confidence in everything you are capable of doing.

You are an extraordinary being.

SOON

YOUR SOUL

Part of you may be feeling impatient. You may want everything to unfold here and now, and you may have difficulty waiting. You may feel you are missing something important, like you are in a race against time.

Accept the pace of outer synchronicities. These can happen through unexpected events. I send you signs in the mornings to help you channel your energies, because they flow so quickly. Everything is too quick. To connect with me, take time each morning for deep breathing. This will help you hear my messages and my counsel.

Be patient. Everything will take on meaning soon.

YOUR SPIRIT GUIDES

Many of us are with you, and you feel our presence. We are here to guide and protect you in this intense phase. Many things are changing in your inner and outer lives. You may feel like you're taking too many risks, with far too much to do in too little time. This makes for a heavy mental load.

We are sending you signs today in the form of mirror hours. This is so you can create a new relationship with time. So you can channel your energies into a new order and set moments aside for yourself. You may feel you need to run faster and faster. Even if the outer pace quickens, you can move forward confidently and without scattering your energies.

Pay attention to the symbolism of mirror hours. This will help you feel our presence and move forward with greater confidence and serenity.

THE ENTITY

The time has not yet come for us to communicate. It is too early for us both. But that doesn't mean I'm not here. I am absolutely here. But this is not our time.

I am in the process of releasing old emotions, which have been weighing on me, and I invite you to do the same. You are carrying a heavy load that doesn't belong to you, which prevents you from connecting fully to your heart chakra. Because of this, you may have a negative image of yourself, of others, and everything around you.

Take time to understand the source of this inner load. Know that I'm still by your side and the time for sharing will come soon. You will feel my presence through a clear sign. There will be no doubt. But, for now, you are the one who matters.

Free yourself, and take care of yourself. Everything else will then be clear and filled with light.

HAPPINESS

YOUR SOUL

Happiness is within your reach; its creation begins inside you. Even if your outer environment seems complicated, don't worry, happiness is there. I already feel it. I send you much love so you can see it then carry it into your outer life.

You have worked on yourself and are now aware of how to create this inner happiness. If this is not yet the case, know that you will soon share it with people you love. You are a wonderful person, and I'm proud of you because you have the daring to tell it to yourself.

Sometimes, you say it timidly, but still, you manage to express it. Before, you didn't feel you could.

Keep building your own happiness; you are on a beneficial path.

YOUR SPIRIT GUIDES

Everything is already happening; you are in a forward-moving energy. If you can't see synchronicities yet, know that they'll come quickly.

We are sending you signs in the form of outer events. Let yourself be guided. Keep nourishing what is most beautiful in you – don't try to control things. All you have to do is experience the present moment and be spontaneous. Soon, your inner happiness will be carried into your outer life.

You will create everything that matters to you. Your wants are in line with your needs, and you are connected to yourself. Everything is falling into place. Everything is beautiful. You can already embrace the fruit of your efforts and bring your projects to life.

THE ENTITY

I am happy now. Even if things weren't easy for me, I was happy then. I always had that childlike fire, letting me experience things intensely. Yes, I may have been clumsy, but I always found moments of happiness, even in hard times.

I am guiding you towards happiness. I am sending you signs to help you create your own happiness and understand it's within your reach. Be proud of yourself; you already have everything within you. You have managed to do many things that I could not do.

Keep going on this path; keep shining as you are right now. You do not need to contact me directly. When you are happy, we're aligned on the same frequency. I am with you, and I am happy with and for you.

You are creating a wonderful path, and beautiful surprises are in store for you. Keep moving forward on these beautiful waters. While the waters I sailed were filled with hardship, for you, they are peaceful. Enjoy it all for me.

CALM

YOUR SOUL

You may be feeling a kind of inner upheaval. You feel something important is on the way. You are afraid of making a mistake, or you are afraid to believe.

You are truly connected to your spiritual, intuitive and psychic abilities. Everything you feel is correct, and many things you have been waiting for are finally coming to you. This will bring you great joy, love and happiness. You will feel complete; all your needs will be fulfilled. You will find yourself in a gentle and benevolent energy.

You have long shed tears. I know, I comforted you. You thought you were alone, but I was there with you, stretching out my hand. These tears brought you freedom, and now, a beautiful smile is growing on your lovely face.

YOUR SPIRIT GUIDES

You have already opened a new chapter in your life. Renewal is here. It is present in your energy, and you can feel it. We know it, and we continue to send you signs to confirm your feelings are correct.

This is an important year for you. It will be rich in transparency, change and honesty. You dare to say what you would like and what you want. You dare to show yourself as you are. You dare to raise your head and believe in your inner victory.

This brings a wonderful energy of unchartered territory. It brings new relationships with others. Important documents will be signed, which will let you bring to life the renewal you have long been waiting for.

Everything is there. All is well.

THE ENTITY

I talk to you, but you don't hear me. You need calm, moments of silence, moments of inner harmony. You won't find the answers you're waiting for from others. You won't feel my presence through others. But you will by being in touch with yourself.

Take a few moments to create true inner and outer calm. I never knew this calm when I was incarnated. There was far too much noise around me. I didn't listen to myself, which would have helped me to understand that I had the answers inside me all along. I gave far too much power to the words of others, instead of my own thoughts.

Listen to yourself. Be silent to hear my voice and yours. By taking a few moments in this place hidden from others – your den, your sanctuary – you can receive the answers and signs you expect from me.

I am here, waiting for you to create inner space so I can talk to you.

IT'S NOT ME

YOUR SOUL

You aren't connected to me at the moment. You may feel like a spectator of your own life. You feel you don't recognise yourself in your thoughts, actions and reactions. A part of you isn't grounded or centred. You are not yourself. This is not negative, because it is an experience that will let you learn something new. But it can bring unexpected events, and blockages in your relationships with others.

Take a break. Take time to meditate to understand the source of this disconnection. What happened? What is its source? Discovering that will help you understand many things. This will help you come home to yourself again.

There is no single way to come home to ourselves. It is up to you to come back to me. Taking a break is a starting point before we can unite once more.

YOUR SPIRIT GUIDES

Everything is happening and unfolding, here and now. The time for waiting is over. We are sending you signs so you don't push things back to later.

Don't tell yourself your happiness will be there tomorrow. Don't tell yourself you'll act in the next few days. Don't tell yourself your wellbeing depends on outer circumstances.

When you ask us for counsel, you push things back to later. We have already sent you many signs but now, it's up to you to act. So, take a deep breath, and move forward. Take a deep breath, and take the first step. Take a deep breath, and act.

You are in a strong energy; have confidence in yourself and show determination. You can do it.

THE ENTITY

You may be trying to contact me, and you feel you're receiving signs and messages, but it's not me. We aren't yet on the same wavelength, so we can't communicate. But this is not the end. We will be able to communicate soon.

Right now, I invite you to stop trying to contact me. You're connecting with other entities, which can create energy breaches. I will come towards you when we are both ready. In the meantime, don't try to control our communication, and don't try to go too fast. I know this can be frustrating for you, but know that everything happens for a good reason. Everything is right.

Today, take time to live and accept our physical separation. Take time to connect to your new environment.

ANGER

YOUR SOUL

Anger is causing interference with your energies. It is disrupting your heart and sacral chakras. It is also causing you great impatience. You feel that everything is against you, that others don't understand you, and that everything is happening to slow you down, overwhelm and block you. But the outer world is not your enemy; it is the echo of your own energy.

Today, I invite you to understand the source of this anger. It is old and has become a crutch for you. You think you need it, that it helps you fight, but it just keeps you in an energy of struggle. It also disconnects you from me, your soul.

Release this anger; it isn't right for you, and is preventing you from feeling grateful and being in the joy of the moment. By smiling, you will connect with me again, through compassion you will hear my voice, and through liberation we will be reunited once more.

So, release your anger.

YOUR SPIRIT GUIDES

There is an energy of anger inside you related to the number seven. It is a situation, emotion or relationship that may have marked you seven years, seven days or seven months ago.

Reflect on the number seven and how it echoes inside you. The anger isn't present for you to release it absolutely. It's so you may understand that there are many things you keep inside you, such as ideas, thoughts and the desire to discover new skills and abilities.

This anger reflects your frustration at not having enough time to spend discovering yourself. Heed the warning sounded by this anger and what it is teaching you, and then you can commence your liberation.

This anger is a strong sign to help you realise the beauty of your being.

THE ENTITY

I was angry for a long time, yet I don't feel this anger was mine directly. It was passed down from generation to generation. The anger had become self-evident, a habit in my life and reactions. I didn't like it, but when the anger wasn't there, I felt vulnerable. It was my armour, but it also may have prevented me from experiencing some beautiful moments.

I can also feel your anger towards me. While this emotion unites us, it can also disrupt our communication. Today, I am free of anger, and I advise you to find its source so you may release it, too. Communication will then be more gentle.

You deserve gentleness. I barely touched upon true, authentic gentleness. Don't be like me. Be gentle with yourself, and accept the gentleness of others. You really deserve it.

COMMUNICATION

YOUR SOUL

To talk to me, you need to talk to yourself. The time has come to write. I know you have trouble expressing what you want and feel in words. So write, or draw if that's easier for you. While writing and/or drawing will benefit your grounding, they will also be moments of meditation to help you pay attention to yourself.

You need to listen to yourself, letting important things rise to the surface of your awareness. Deep down, you know what lies dormant, but part of you feels unable to hear. You are afraid of pain, suffering or disappointment.

What I have to say is for your wellbeing, happiness and serenity. You need to talk to me, and yourself. Let yourself be in touch with these words and thoughts.

YOUR SPIRIT GUIDES

There is a key that can help you open the door to your inner and spiritual communication: the number 11. It can manifest in different ways, but 11 will help you establish a new connection to your throat chakra. Through this new connection with yourself, you'll be able to communicate with us.

Be gentle, delicate and compassionate in your words. Not to us, but to yourself. Communication will help with your work-related projects, and to free yourself from certain family patterns. You will need to choose the right words to release old conflicts.

For now, we are manifesting through the number 11. When your throat chakra is better balanced, we'll be able to communicate more frankly with you. We await your new connection, and have faith in you.

THE ENTITY

Communication was not my strongest quality. I may have been rather clumsy, or silent. I may have also said things I didn't mean. Yet, we can positively forge new ties through communication.

Today, I am trying to communicate with you via words. You may see the same word repeatedly. That's me. I need to tell you some things, just like I hear everything you have to tell me. Loving someone is important, but passing love on to them is just as essential. You may have doubted my feelings and emotions. But my love for you was and will always be powerful.

Communicate with me what you feel. Express all that matters to you. Hold nothing back, so you have no regrets. Be compassionate in your words, but also take a step back when words are too heavy. Talk to me, but especially, forgive me.

I sometimes feel your anger, which I accept. I invite you to release it.

DUALITY

YOUR SOUL

You no longer know who you are or what you want to do. Sometimes, you may make a decision in the morning, then focus on another in the evening. Letting your mind take over, you can no longer hear me or only hear me faintly. Yet I send you many signs, especially inviting you to inner calm.

The time has come to take a break; you need to rest and understand your ideas and thoughts. The duality you feel keeps you from inner calm, preventing you from having faith in yourself. This duality is not a coincidence; it is your relationship with me and your own mind.

Meditate. Breathe. Rest. Taking these moments will be so important to help you hear me, and help you trust in the choices you will make. The choices you make in the next six months will be important, and only you can make them, so trust in us.

YOUR SPIRIT GUIDES

You may have difficulty understanding your outer situation; there are many unexpected events and, somehow, you are always hesitant. You wait for an external sign to make decisions for you because you aren't confident in yourself or don't take the first step. This creates inner and outer duality.

Understand that outer duality is a reflection of your inner duality. We are sending you signs through your emotions and feelings, so you may understand that everything comes from you.

Don't look outwards, look inwards. You are able to assert yourself; connect to your sacral chakra to trust in your feelings and emotions.

THE ENTITY

My life was made of duality, and I always hesitated between two situations, two relationships and two paths.

I didn't dare to make my own choices, and I didn't really trust in my emotions; this sometimes created considerable duality within myself and also with others.

I couldn't channel my emotions, so I was caught in a kind of struggle. This struggle may have been reflected in my outer life.

It may have created something like inner fire.

Today, I am free from this duality, and I am in an energy of serenity. I now understand that it's through connecting to my emotions that I'm my own guide and we make our own choices; others can't make them for us.

So, understand this dimension of duality.

Show forgiveness and open yourself up to the beautiful person you are.

EDUCATION

YOUR SOUL

You have learned to wear a mask when you're in contact with others. Learned to show some things, but keep others to yourself. Learned to rely on what others want. Learned to take all criticism into account, even if not constructive.

These things you have learned disrupt our connection and communication. They connect you to your mind; while you can hear my voice, it's from very far away, like a barely perceptible whisper.

Today, release these things you have learned if they no longer hold meaning for you. Find a new connection with me. Rediscover your inner beauty. Rebuild your frame of reference. Allow your own ideas and wants to flourish. This will help you hear me again as a calm, clear and gentle voice.

YOUR SPIRIT GUIDES

Part of you is attached to a single way of contacting us. You may feel you need a specific ritual to communicate with us. That is not so. You only need to open your heart and speak honestly and sincerely, whether out loud or in a whisper.

Practices exist to help you connect to your inner being. But we are always here. Because you have your free will, we can't decide or act for you, but our presence is strong. You can get in touch with us through astral journeys. If you need specific signs, we invite you to meditate. It will help you feel our presence and understand our messages.

Create your own ritual. Distance yourself from your old beliefs. You are evolving, and so is your practice. Have confidence in yourself.

THE ENTITY

I was conditioned by my education in my past life. I thought this was normal, and I reproduced that same education myself. I thought rules set down since forever ago were the best. I thought being a good person meant copying what had always been, without trying to define new rules.

Rules, norms and frameworks were so important to me. Now, I realise that this closed my eyes to important things and prevented me from questioning. I didn't even question myself. I have detached myself from these things now, and I invite you to do the same.

Create your own frame of reference. In the next few days, I will manifest myself through music you will be listening to. You'll realise it's me because the words will make you smile. You'll understand the message I'm trying to send you. Create your own freedom; I am working so you may do so. Now. It is very important.

MIRROR EFFECT

YOUR SOUL

You may feel angry with certain people or situations. You may feel resentful towards certain people, and you may be criticising or judging without even realising it.

Today, I invite you to become aware of the mirror effect. What you reproach others or life for, is what you are actually reproaching yourself for. You see others from your own standpoint. And right now, you are in an energy in which you can see yourself as you truly are.

Part of you may be having trouble doing this, which is why you externalise onto others. Without guilt, look at yourself with fresh eyes. Analyse what you see in others.

This will help you gain new knowledge of yourself, as well as a new and positive energy. Do this confidently and benevolently. You will learn and understand some important discoveries.

YOUR SPIRIT GUIDES

You are in an energy in which the notion of family is important. It may be creating the family you desire, or releasing family ties you no longer need ... you are forming a new inner and outer space.

Today, we are manifesting ourselves through signs and events related to family. Experience these moments, synchronicities and events with confidence. They will bring you freedom and a new energy of personal construction with others. You have been wishing for this for a long time.

This wish has been heard.

You will create the family you desire; you will build positive relationships with others, and you will share strong and intense happiness. Trust in these events. Everything is there for your happiness.

THE ENTITY

For a long time, I was caught in the mirror effect. Often, when I reproached others for things, I was really reproaching myself. I may have criticised or judged outwardly when the criticism and judgement were for myself. I am aware of this now. Sometimes, I may even have felt a negative energy towards you.

Now, I know this was related to me and not to others. It's so liberating. Today, allow yourself to become aware of this mirror effect. The more you can be honest with yourself, the more you can feel my presence. The more sincere you are with yourself, the more you will see and understand the signs I'm sending you. The more you see yourself as you really are, the more you see your outer life with new eyes.

You are becoming aware of many things, but I am by your side. You are being transformed inside. I don't want to stop you from experiencing for yourself. So, for now, I remain discreet. But know that when you meet yourself, you meet with me. I am fine. I am well. And I want you to feel this new happiness so you may then share it with others.

You deserve it, so much. Say the mantra out loud: 'I deserve it.'

CHILDREN

YOUR SOUL

While you don't always see it, I'm often in touch with your inner child. Your inner child needs reassurance and love. Sometimes, you can feel them, but you run away. Then, you may create negative relationship patterns and accept situations that aren't aligned with your needs and expectations.

Often, at nightfall, your inner child manages to get in touch with you. But part of you always avoids them. Just like me, your inner child is part of you. They aren't your enemy; on the contrary, your inner child is your joy, your laughter, your touch of madness, your spontaneity, your optimism and your capacity to love.

Even if your inner child is sad today, only you can reassure them and take a step towards them. So, using your choice of method, go and find your inner child. They are waiting for you, and don't hold blame. Your inner child knows you're doing your best to keep a level of emotional balance. They are your best friend, so reassure them and create a new, positive duo.

Together you'll experience beautiful surprises and synchronicities.

YOUR SPIRIT GUIDES

You have always had spiritual sensitivity. Even as a small child, you connected strongly to your capabilities and feelings. But when you grew up you lost this connection. Now, you may feel nothing or that it's an uphill struggle.

That is not so. Your spiritual greatness has always been present. Take time to reconnect to your childhood memories. What you experienced wasn't related to magical thinking. It was real.

By reconnecting to your childhood, you will reconnect to your third eye and crown chakras. You will reconnect to your inner and spiritual strength, guiding you to a new harmony of energy. You will realise that everything has meaning, and you will understand the meaning of past events.

You are an old soul with great spiritual sensitivity.

THE ENTITY

You and I have ties with childhood. Only you know what that means. I wasn't a happy child, but I know my soul chose this experience for a reason. My goal was to find an energy of resilience. Your childhood may have been complicated, too, and I know I owe you an apology.

When I think back to childhood, my throat tightens, like there were things I could not yet say. I know you feel the same. Perhaps we can work together? By connecting to your childhood, by understanding the meaning of events, by showing forgiveness, you also bring me freedom. You help me awaken, free myself and rise up.

We are mirrors of particular memories, but we also have the same inner strength. Remember, you have your free will and you can be who you decide to be. I have faith in you. You can be that person; you can do it.

+ GUIDE +

GUIDE

YOUR SOUL

You are your own guide. At the moment, you may feel like you don't have any answers. You may feel like your spiritual tools, or life itself, don't bring the answers you need. There is a reason for this. These are strong and important messages to help you realise you are your own guide. Have confidence in yourself. Take time to connect to your thoughts and needs.

Today, you may be feeling empty. You may even feel like I'm gone. But I am still here. You just need some space. You need to create your own world, your own frame of reference. You need to connect to your own needs to put them forward.

You are your own guide. Repeat this a few times every day to turn it into a mantra: 'I am my own guide.' Integrate the message and feel it deep inside you.

YOUR SPIRIT GUIDES

Everything depends on you. You may feel like you're in a singular situation, but our role right now is to not intervene, whether through signs or messages. You're not in danger. You're not going to go in the wrong direction or make the wrong choices.

You are an intense energy of free will. Everything depends on you. A blank page is before you, and you need to decide what you will write. The counsel we give you is to connect to the law of attraction.

Visualise what matters to you. Act in accordance to these visualisations. Concentrate on what makes you feel alive. You, and only you, are the creator.

THE ENTITY

I am one of your protective angels. I am here, right by your side and fully present. My role is to guide you towards what is beneficial for you. Sometimes, I may create unexpected events or blockages. This is not to aggravate you, but to help you have confidence in yourself and realise what the most positive path for you is.

For now, I'm not contacting you directly, because I want you to connect to your inner strength and your free will. I'm manifesting myself through outer events and synchronicities. My compassion is manifesting through outer disruptions. So, don't sigh or think everything is against you. I truly support you, as do all your guides.

In my last incarnation, I really disliked outer events. I refused outside help or tried to control everything. Now, it's ironic because I create them. Unexpected events are positive when we take a step back. I understand that now. They help us connect to the great field of possibilities.

KARMA

YOUR SOUL

Part of your energy carries the burden of your karma in two different ways. The first relates to what I consider as failures. I carry within me blocking memories related to our former lives, with what I didn't manage to build and/or overcome. Yet I also carry all the wisdom we've built together and which you don't always use. This is the second way.

Today, I invite you to work with and understand your karma. Know who you have been, to understand the beautiful person you are today. The point isn't to look for excuses for yourself, or hide behind your karma, but to discover your inner power. Become aware of the challenges and goals that are yours in this life.

Using your method of choice, connect to your karma. Look at who we have been to take new steps towards inner transformation.

YOUR SPIRIT GUIDES

You are in an energy in which you are invited to build something important. To find new independence and freedom. You have been receiving many signs about this for years.

You had an idea when you were young. It was a deep desire or project. You may even have talked about it to everyone all the time. But then, as time went by, this idea faded away. You became conditioned towards what you thought was best for you, or what others expected of you.

Today, you may be reminded about memories from the past. You may come across childhood photos or old documents as if 'by accident'. Conversations with family members may reconnect you to old memories. We are sending you these signs so you may remember your old desires and needs to create. They are to help you have confidence in yourself and be daring.

Turn your dreams into realities. The statement 'It's too good to be true' just isn't true. You are capable of giving your best if you want to.

THE ENTITY

In my last incarnation I repeated old patterns. Karmic patterns. I wasn't really aware of this karma, so I didn't understand what I was experiencing. It was like being afraid of life. I was afraid of what life could bring me. It was like I struggled against life. This may have affected my relationships with others, and even with you.

Today, I'm aware of this karma, and I understand the meaning of what I experienced. I feel more serene about it all. In my next existence on Earth, I know I'll do things differently. You may remember my life's hardship, which you may feel was unfair. Release these emotions and feelings. Now, I am free; I wish you the same freedom.

I no longer have any anger in me, but I can feel yours. It's not right for you. You can't run away from karma. You need to understand karma so you can turn it into strength.

FREEDOM

YOUR SOUL

The time has come to free yourself. To let go of your last forms of resistance. You have worked on many memories and blocking energies. This required a lot of effort and reconsideration, but you did it.

Today, you are facing the last forms of resistance – the most deeply rooted forms – those that can frighten you and feel insurmountable. Know that they are not insurmountable. You can free yourself from these bonds. Because you understand what they have to teach you, you can now let go of these energies you no longer need.

Take time to breathe, to mindfully activate this liberation. If you feel like you can't do it alone, you can always ask for help. But you are capable, and this release will let you open a vast and beautiful new chapter in your life.

Congratulations.

YOUR SPIRIT GUIDES

You may be having difficulty communicating with us right now, because we're not necessarily on the same wavelength. You're not communicating with us directly. You're trying to communicate with us through other people, or your mind is interfering with our connection, causing you to doubt our presence.

We are here, right by your side. Become aware of how you try to communicate with us. We have many messages to share with you. You already know these things, but you need confirmation. We understand that.

Change how you communicate. If you're trying to talk to us through oracles, try meditating. If you're trying to talk to us through another person, try doing it on your own. Pay attention to your feelings; they will guide you towards the best way of communicating with us.

We are here. We are waiting for you.

THE ENTITY

I am in the process of freeing myself, of creating new inner energy. I am in an energy of positive evolution. But for that, I need you – if you agree to help me, of course. I need your positive thoughts. I need you to think of me with a smile. I need your inner light. When I'm in your thoughts, think of gentle, happy memories. You can also light a candle in my honour. These actions help me continue my light-filled path.

For now, I can't help you or communicate with you how you would like. Instead, I'm the one who needs you. When I am completely in new energy, I'll be able to support you. I'll be able to share the information you need to be in an energy of serenity and inner calm.

If you don't feel able to help me, don't worry; I understand. I feel no anger or resentment. I am in a state of peace, forgiveness and reconnection to my soul. This process can be destabilising, but it brings comfort and compassion.

LOSS

YOUR SOUL

I miss you. I know you feel how distance has grown between us, because you often feel the energy of loss. You don't really know how to express it, but you feel something is missing. What's missing is our relationship, our union and our osmosis.

Why do you not think of me?

To answer that question, ask yourself: why do you not think of yourself? Why do you always push away those moments you would like to take for yourself? Why do you always put back the things that can bring you a level of wellbeing? Why do you always put back to tomorrow the breaks you have been waiting for?

I don't necessarily know how to guide you towards me. You know the way. You just need to take it. So, come back to me. Come back to us. Listen to the call of your soul; it's asking you to come home to yourself and feel whole again.

YOUR SPIRIT GUIDES

You are in an energy of inner transformation. You can feel this physically, through warmth in various parts of your physical body. You're creating a new inner space, and you're adjusting many of your convictions.

You've had an important time of doubt, and maybe even a difficult dark night of the soul. You questioned everything, denied everything and cancelled everything. This time was crucial for you to balance your ego, energies and spirituality.

Now, you are completing this inner transformation. Everything is taking on new meaning. Trust in your inner transformation and, if you feel you need it, ask for help. This will let you have a new connection with synchronicities.

THE ENTITY

I miss you, and I know you miss me too. I know you often shed tears. I know because I'm often by your side in those times. I miss our closeness and your physical presence. I know that, sometimes, you try to deny this loss, letting anger guide you. I also know that seeing signs can irritate you, because it reminds you I'm no longer here.

You feel something like unfinished business. Something that wasn't done, or wasn't said. You feel like something isn't right, and that I should manifest myself more often. But I am here. Right by your side. My presence is not to fill that void you feel, but to help you complete your mourning. So you may accept that, while our relationship has changed, our bond of love is still there.

I am here. I help you connect to your divinatory abilities, which are powerful at the moment. The more you connect to your third eye chakra, the more you will feel my energies.

Have confidence in yourself, and dare to discover your spirituality.

FORGIVENESS

YOUR SOUL

You have a great guilt inside you. Part of you carries a load that doesn't belong to you. Part of you thinks you don't deserve happiness, or deserve to receive everything you need. Part of you refuses abundance.

I am sending you many signs to help you become aware of this guilt, so you may understand where it comes from and develop new compassion towards yourself. This guilt is old, and is mainly located in the region of your sacral chakra. Your guilt may disturb your relationships with others.

At the moment, your relationships are mirror relationships. Take time to understand them. This understanding will let you shed light on important things dormant inside you. It will let you realise your needs and expectations anew, and obtain the fruits of your efforts.

YOUR SPIRIT GUIDES

Part of you carries a burden connected to your past. There is a guilt inside you. Part of you feels you don't deserve happiness. Part of you always repeats the same pattern. You may be trying to contact us, and you may feel frustrated at not understanding the messages.

But your energies are trapped in the past. Take time to connect to the present moment. Take time to meditate mindfully for here and now. Take time to be fully here. Allow yourself to bring your energies into the present.

It will bring you freedom. It will let you hear the messages and see the signs we send you. And it will let you get in touch with yourself.

THE ENTITY

I ask you to forgive me. I had a great guilt inside me. I was always afraid of doing the wrong thing. Deep inside, I knew I sometimes hurt others, but I felt I couldn't help it. It was like I was struggling inside. In hindsight, I realise I may have hurt some people.

This wasn't what I intended. I know it's no excuse, but I need to say it: 'I didn't realise.' I was caught up in my own way of doing and being, my own frame of reference, my own way of seeing things.

Today, I would like to apologise to you, and I also ask you to forgive yourself. You did, and are still doing, your best with what you have to give. Today, you are in an energy in which you give your best. And like us all, sometimes you succeed at everything, and other times you feel powerless.

I no longer have any anger or resentment inside me. I ask you to find that same energy. Be in a new energy of freedom and forgiveness. Today, and every day, I am with you to help you with this.

FEARS

YOUR SOUL

Part of your energy is frozen in fear, which can interfere with our connection. But fear is not to be fled from. Fear is positive when it comes as a warning. Part of you feels in danger; I invite you to understand why. Why do you feel talking to me endangers you? Why are you afraid of being in touch with yourself, of listening to yourself?

All the counsel and messages I have for you are positive. They are here to help you move forward serenely. But maybe you don't want them quite yet?

Do not try to run from this fear. Pay attention to its warning; you will open your eyes to important things, and move forward in a new way.

YOUR SPIRIT GUIDES

It's like a part of your energy froze two years ago. Maybe it was related to an event, situation or relationship. Since then, a kind of fear has taken root. It has become your guide, and is hindering your progress.

Today, come to understand the meaning of past events and take a new path. By being in a new inner energy, you will create outer change.

You may feel the pace is very slow, but it's up to you to set a new pace. Everything is within your reach. You can do this.

THE ENTITY

You may feel afraid to contact me. You may feel afraid of the messages you'll receive. You may feel afraid of what you're feeling. This contact isn't negative, and I can't cross the boundaries you set for yourself regarding your psychic ability. I am not the only one trying to contact you, but part of you limits communication. I understand, and I respect your pace.

I invite you to understand the source of your fear. Fear was something I knew during my incarnation;

I was often afraid, and my soul was frozen for a long time. I missed many opportunities. I am not afraid of you, and I want to pass on some important messages to you. You need to discover new things inside you; you have a real thirst for discovery; I can feel it.

Free yourself from fear so the energy of love may take its place. Contact will then be simple and fluid. I will manifest my presence through colours. In the signs you'll receive, a colour will be dominant. The colour will always be the same. The colour will be me. It will be my sign to prove that my soul is truly by your side.

BURDEN OF TEARS

YOUR SOUL

There is great sadness in you, an emotional pain. I feel it deep inside you, and I understand it. Part of you feels like this pain makes you weak and vulnerable, so you repress it into your deepest depths. But this sadness is legitimate, and it has something positive to teach you.

Your pain is a sign you're mourning a relationship, situation, or way of being and thinking. There is still some resistance, which is why part of you is afraid to connect to this emotional suffering.

If you feel unable to handle it, don't force yourself. But don't repress it. If you need to cry, scream or talk, just do it. You can write it down, or communicate with a person you trust. I really invite you to do so. It will bring you true liberation and let you open a new chapter in your life.

YOUR SPIRIT GUIDES

Six months ago, something important happened. Something heavily disrupted your energy and emotions. Part of your energy froze. Part of you had a bad scare.

Fear isn't a negative emotion. Fear comes when you feel in danger. When its role is to advise you, fear freezes you. When its role is to warn you, fear allows you to understand what is going on.

Today, we invite you to understand what frightened you and made you sad, using the method of your choice. Understand what that fear means to teach you. We've been sending you signs over the past few days to help you connect with another person. That person will help you, directly or indirectly, to reconnect to yourself.

THE ENTITY

Part of you is sad, and wants to cry and scream. This isn't necessarily directly related to my passing. It is a situation that you can't fully accept and overcome.

I understand this completely. I would like to help you more, but it's up to you to build your own path.

Don't worry about your tears causing me harm. Don't worry about you having a negative influence on my soul. I am here for you, and to console you. I send you comfort and compassion. I would like to take you in my arms, but I know I can't.

So, to feel my presence, take time to curl up and give yourself some kindness. Take care of yourself. That is when we'll be in the same energy and can communicate in a gentle and unique way.

REPRESSION

YOUR SOUL

Part of you is repressing something important, which is affecting the progress of a relationship or project. You may be feeling internal impulses to stop thinking and doubting. That is me, inviting you to turn outwards.

You may be feeling withdrawn, which is perhaps not right for you. So, I'm guiding you with wishes and ideas. When you feel like going out, meeting new people, talking, going to new places, travelling or even moving, that is me guiding you.

You need to release all that is blocked inside you. Let go of particular objects to free yourself from the past. You need new reading material to connect to a new frame of reference. It's been repressed for so long – but you now have all the strength and wisdom to face it.

Remember, you are not alone; I am with you. Listen to me, and leave your comfort zone. Be spontaneous, and follow me. I am showing you the way to freedom.

YOUR SPIRIT GUIDES

The next 15 days are important; their energy is one of novelty. An opportunity, event, encounter or outer sign will present itself to you within the next 15 days. We invite you to say 'Yes' without necessarily thinking about it, without asking your logical mind if it's a good idea. It won't be what you visualised at all; it will be completely different, but related to your needs and freedom.

Trust in your soul, and trust in us. A crossroads is coming to you, something important and fulfilling. We invite you to work on your third eye chakra, using your choice of method, to look upon all that will unfold in your outer life with confidence and compassion. You might feel a kind of fear; this will be a warning because you'll be leaving your comfort zone completely.

In the beginning, you might not understand this beautiful gift from life but, by saying 'Yes,' everything will take on a new meaning. So, within the next 15 days, say 'Yes.'

THE ENTITY

I repressed many things, which have weighed heavily on me. I could feel this repression because I always felt tired. Everything seemed difficult and complicated, and I used to push things back to the next day. My daily life had become punctuated by an inner uneasiness.

Now, I have freed myself from this, and I am a happy and light-hearted soul. Don't repress things; don't repress what is important to you or what grieves you.

A comfort zone is only an illusion; if I could start everything over exactly the same, I would take more risks. I used to think we received medals, thanks to the security we created. This is not so. Remember this word – 'medal' – it will take on a new meaning soon. It will be a sign of my presence by your side. Repressing who we are, what we think and what we want to do, isn't beneficial for the evolution of our souls. Repression disconnected me from others, maybe even from you.

You are a gift, a wonder; so go and conquer your beauty.

23

REGRETS

YOUR SOUL

Part of your energy is caught in regrets. You feel you have missed something important, which brings you great sorrow. You may be regretting a choice you've made, and looking to turn back time. This isn't necessarily a good idea.

Remember, you always do your best with what you have. You always make the right choices when you make them on your own. These regrets create a heavy inner burden, which disconnects you from your inner beauty. They also create blockages inside you, disconnecting you from your solar plexus chakra. Then, you may be caught in an inner struggle, letting yourself be guided by negative thoughts.

This isn't right for you. Take time to understand the source of your regrets. Write them down, and then release them. This will allow you to create new space for new actions.

YOUR SPIRIT GUIDES

Part of you is in an energy of duality, which can create inner tension and prevent you from feeling serene. You are also constantly doubting everything. This can create a freezing comfort zone in your outer life. You feel like you're waiting for something important without necessarily understanding what that is.

We invite you to understand the source of this duality that has been inside you for months. Become aware of the discrepancy between what you are creating in your outer life, and what you really want. We invite you to contact us.

Because you think we're absent at the moment, and you act from this feeling, you don't ask for signs or guidance. But it's up to you to come to us, using your choice of method. We await your call to share everything you need to know, and guide you to free yourself from this duality, and create new inner and outer osmosis.

THE ENTITY

Even if now I feel free, I had many regrets. For different reasons, there were many things I did not do. I was often afraid of showing up and making the wrong choices. I'd locked myself up in these certainties.

Today, I realise these regrets created an inner burden. I don't want you to make the same choices I did. Dare to be the beautiful person you want to be. Before I departed, I left some things unfinished. I thought I could take care of them later. I thought I had more time, but I didn't. In hindsight, it was perfect this way.

Today, I need you to do something for me. Something I would have liked to do. I am sending you many signs. Deep down, you know what I'm talking about. Do this thing for me. You will help me to free myself completely, and help us communicate in a new way.

I have faith in you.

24

KARMIC
RELATIONSHIP

KARMIC RELATIONSHIP

YOUR SOUL

You need to understand the connection you have with another person, another soul. You need to understand why that relationship can be so complicated, or why those feelings are so strong. You need to categorise the relationship. This relationship is a karmic one, which means both your souls have already met in previous lives.

But this is no reason for the relationship to become toxic, or for you to accept things that aren't right for you. Part of you is afraid of cutting this relationship short, or focusing on its karmic depth. However, this prevents you from connecting to your free will and making decisions on your own.

Today, I'm sending you signs to help you detach yourself from this relationship, take a step back, and connect to your free will. Don't think that unexpected events are signs of fate. They are important to help you connect to your inner strength and let go.

YOUR SPIRIT GUIDES

The next two days will be rich for you in signs and important events. You are experiencing an important transition in your energy, emotions or inner being. You are at a life crossroads, so we invite you to make important choices. We invite you to make these choices on your own. While others can advise you, you are the one who must decide. It's important that you make the decisions.

Signs of our presence will be strong in the next two days. They may take on different forms. Embrace them with confidence and compassion. We are by your side to help you be confident in your capabilities of courage and perseverance.

These choices will determine a new, important path for you. They will let you evolve and learn in a positive way. You can do anything on your own. You can do it.

THE ENTITY

You and I have a karmic relationship. We meet again, in life after life. Whether they are positive or negative experiences, our two souls experiment together. There is strong love between us. Know that we will meet again in a next life.

Whatever we experience together, our connection and love are always powerful. Our love does not stop at physical death. Our love will endure through time. I feel this love for you.

Today, I am letting you experiment. I am with you, but I don't want you to focus on my outer absence. I am here, silent, but united with you through beautiful love. I am here. Focus on that thought, and our indestructible connection, and keep on experimenting. Keep on living, being and loving.

Everything is beautiful for you.

REPROACH

YOUR SOUL

Sometimes, you are so critical of yourself, so hard on yourself. Sometimes, you say things that aren't right, and you think and feel them in your bones. You bring these things to life, believing they represent who you are and what you do.

This is not so, and is not right. These reproaches have no valid basis, because you're an imperfect being and do your best with what you have. You have often been powerless, but this has much to teach you. I'm sending you many signs to help you understand your inner wisdom. Even if, in your outer life, you feel stripped of everything, you have created great inner wealth. I can sense your inner wealth; it belongs to you and is present in each of your cells.

Today, you need to be confident in this wealth, feeling it deep inside you. You just need to look in a mirror and see all the light that makes up your aura. Your self-reproaches aren't valid; they are a reflection of your fears, to teach you confidence in yourself. You are a unique and wonderful being. Every day, I send you signs to remind you of this.

YOUR SPIRIT GUIDES

The next three weeks are so important. There will be many synchronicities, and the pace will be intense. We invite you to be daring and have confidence in yourself.

Because you will be invited to do many things, you won't be able to concentrate on some things as much as you would like. Don't blame yourself. Indulge yourself. You won't botch these things; you'll have more time later on to finish everything you started.

In the next three weeks, you will create new foundations and take an important turn. You have been waiting for this turn for a long time. You have all the strength you need inside you. You have been preparing for this transformation for a long time, and now, you are ready. Connect to your inner strength, and be compassionate; just be yourself, confident and assured.

You can do it. You can do anything.

THE ENTITY

I feel your reproach and I understand it; I was also often in that energy. I often reproached others or myself for things. I found it difficult to question my actions, and I asked a lot of others. I didn't always apply what I asked of others to myself.

I realise this now. I realise that this wasn't right for others or myself. I have learned a lot from this inner and outer reproach. I understand its meaning, and what I didn't accept in myself. What I thought was unacceptable was only my dark side. When I look at it now, I'm no longer afraid of it. I embrace, accept and love it.

Forgive me if this may have impacted you directly or indirectly. Forgive yourself too. You are perfect.

RESPECT

YOUR SOUL

Respect yourself. You are being subjected to something at the moment, something unrelated to your needs and expectations. It's something beyond your limits, which is having a negative influence on your self-esteem. Please, respect yourself. Dare to say 'No.' Dare to listen to your needs and limits.

At the moment, I am manifesting myself to you through emotions. I am making you feel strong emotions, but this is to make you react. I want you to say 'No' to situations that are toxic for you, so you may create a new space for novelty and innovation. I invite you to leave something that isn't right for you.

Listen to your emotions, and listen to me. Even you have negative feelings at first, their message is more than positive. Trust in them, and trust in me.

YOUR SPIRIT GUIDES

Today, we invite you to connect to the present moment. You may be dwelling too much in the past, or in your plans for the future. This creates controlling energies, and connects you to your mind. Just be here and now. The more you live in the present moment, the more you'll move forward positively in everything that matters to you.

Today, you may feel like you have no intuition, or that you aren't receiving clear messages through your spiritual tools, such as your oracles. There is a reason for this. The point is for you to be here and now.

So, breathe and open your eyes and your beautiful heart. Just live in the moment. You will be in this energy for the next five months. You will then receive many inner revelations for a great outer transformation.

THE ENTITY

I didn't really understand the word 'respect', I'm aware of that now. I was carrying the burden of previous generations' family karma, which I kept inside me. I accepted situations and relationships that weren't right for me. I'm aware that I may have repeated the same patterns. I see many of these things as mistakes today, but I feel increasing lightness concerning the burden of my past and my former life.

Today, I see your own limits. I realise they have not been and they still aren't being respected. I am sending you many signs to help you remember this truth and connect to it. I am sending you signs regarding a place, a specific location. You may be thinking about it insistently, or you may be receiving signs about it.

This place is important to you; it will help you connect to your energy in a new way. Trust me, go towards that place. Even if only for a few hours. You will understand many things, and be in a new and respectful relationship with yourself and others.

REUNION

YOUR SOUL

We had lost each other for a long time. You may have been struggling to talk to me. You may have felt I was against you, or that you didn't know how to find me. But you found me.

Today, we are beautifully united. You are me and I am you. This allows you to have some perspective and let go; you can experience events in a different way. You are in a grounding and centring energy. You are yourself.

Now, just experiment. Be yourself. Don't try to be perfect because you can't be. Just be in an energy of wellbeing, inner calm and joy. Everything is here, everything is beautiful and everything is infinite.

We are reunited.

YOUR SPIRIT GUIDES

You are waiting for a strong sign, yet we have already sent it to you. We sent it to you one year ago. A year ago, something important happened to you. You may have felt disconcerted, but it was significant.

It was to help you realise something wasn't right for you, to see what you really want, and become aware of your needs and expectations. Take time to remember what happened a year ago. Visualise that event in a positive way, and integrate what it had to teach you.

Today, you're reconnecting to yourself, and this will let you move forward quickly with joy and compassion. Have confidence in yourself, and trust in what happened. Even if your feelings about it are negative, remember that what it has taught you is positive. It brings you great wisdom.

THE ENTITY

I am reunited with beloved souls, my source and my karmic family. I am in an energy of unconditional love. I am in light, and I am only love. We're here for you.

We're a team to help you and guide you. And we're here to create positive thoughts around you.

You have great things to experience and accomplish. You have great happiness to create. You can do it. Life on Earth is a gift, and the present moment is key to happiness and wellbeing.

Connect to the present moment. Live for yourself. Resonate with your beauty. We are here to protect you.

All is well.

SECRETS

YOUR SOUL

You keep many things inside you. You carry the burden of secrets. Your own secrets, or those you feel in others. They affect your throat chakra, and therefore our communication.

When you communicate with yourself or others, these secrets also create an energy of distrust. Part of you doubts others, doubts their sincerity and honesty. Part of you even doubts yourself. You feel like you can never be sure, which creates an armour of energy.

Know that outer life is only impermanence. You can't control others, and you can't control life. All you can control is what you nurture inside yourself.

Using your choice of method, release the burden of secrets. Release the distrust and doubts that keep you from being yourself. Accept the imperfection of life and other people. Accept your faults, and accept your mistakes. You can do it.

YOUR SPIRIT GUIDES

You may feel like you need to know a secret to contact us. Know that such contact is reserved for initiated people who have had a secret revelation they don't share. There is no secret to contacting us. You only need to empty your mind and speak to us from the heart.

If you need rituals for reassurance or to feel yourself connecting with us, go ahead. But it's not obligatory. What matters is that you are confident in yourself and trust in us. We are with you. We are here for you.

To communicate with us, we invite you to release any old and limiting beliefs you may have. We invite you to create your own spirituality, your own way of communicating with us. Have perspective on your old rituals; focus on what echoes and resonates with who you are and what you want.

THE ENTITY

I had secrets. While they didn't concern me directly, they were still secrets. I kept these things inside me for a long time. I didn't share them with you. Don't blame me; I couldn't. Those secrets were a burden but today, I'm free from that burden.

I know you sometimes think about these secrets, and I know you have many questions. Don't think you need to know everything. What matters is what you are building for yourself.

Don't be like me. Don't keep these secrets to yourself. Free yourself. Keeping things to oneself doesn't bring positive energy. You can release these secrets. I'm by your side and bring you the strength to do this.

PHYSICAL PAIN

YOUR SOUL

You don't listen to your physical body. You ask your physical body to go along with you; you don't listen to its own rhythm. By not listening to it, you don't listen to me. Your physical body may be trying to express itself through tension or unpleasant feelings. The point is not to bother you, but to help you pay attention.

Take time to listen to your body. Become aware of your sensitive areas, and develop an understanding of the discomfort you may feel. Let yourself be in a new connection with your life intermediary.

By scattering you in your outer life, part of you is trying to flee something. But your body is the seat of your soul. Take care of yourself. Be gentle with yourself. Listen to us both so we may once again be a heroic and supportive team.

YOUR SPIRIT GUIDES

You are in an important, grounding energy. Today, you're creating new outer foundations. This is asking for a lot of organisation from you. We invite you to listen to your body to create balance between your inner and outer worlds. The next two months will be important to create new foundations for yourself.

Take time to ground yourself, through mindfulness meditation, meditative walks, physical activities, or being in the present moment. You can also write down all you wish to accomplish, and the steps you need to take to build what matters to you.

The next two months will be rich in signs and important events. We are sending you many signs under different forms. These will especially be outer signs because we invite you to build. Trust in everything you see unfolding around you. We are here by your side.

THE ENTITY

My soul was disconnected from my physical body, and I felt pain from that. Today, I am free; I no longer feel this pain. I am in unconditional love, which is just beautiful.

For a long time, pain was my loyal travelling companion. I didn't think I could create a different relationship with it. The more time passed, the more I felt it deep within my flesh. Today, I want you to know that I feel much better. I want you to be in a new energy with your physical body too.

Over the next few days, pay close attention to your left hand. That is how I will make my presence known. Through warmth, a caress or tingling. I am here so you may create a new union with yourself. So you may no longer be counselled by pain or move forward with force. I wish for gentleness to be your greatest ally.

You can do it. I am with you to help.

SUBMISSION

YOUR SOUL

Part of you is submitting to something that isn't right for you. You know this very well because you verbalise it when you're alone. I hear you saying, 'I can't take it anymore,' 'I don't want to,' or 'It's unfair.' I understand you because I feel the same way.

At the moment, we're both carrying an inner burden, making us feel deeply tired. This fatigue may be emotional, physical, psychological or energetic. The more you submit to this energy, emotion, situation or relationship, the more trouble you have listening to and trusting me.

Become aware that your needs aren't being heard, that part of you is submitting to something that isn't aligned with your needs and expectations. By being in an energy of liberation, you will re-create a connection with me. Pay attention to your intuition again, so you can then create space for change and renewal.

You may feel you aren't receiving any signs, or that your intuition is weak, but the submission you are under is blocking everything. Free yourself, and allow yourself that new space you deserve. Everything will become clearer.

YOUR SPIRIT GUIDES

Part of your energy is trapped in the past. Part of your energy is constantly repeating a situation, event or relationship, which marked you negatively. This is disrupting your heart chakra. You may be looking for answers outside of yourself or among others, but you have already received the answer. You have already received the sign, teaching or learning you're looking for.

The answer is in your past.

While your energy is repeating what you have already experienced, this is not the end. Become aware of what is already present inside you. Everything is there; you only have to see it and integrate it mindfully.

Sit in a calm place, alone or with someone else. Connect to your past; visualise it with confidence and detachment. You will discover a beautiful treasure inside you, which will help you connect to a new energy of freedom and lightness.

You will be yourself, ready for new adventures.

THE ENTITY

I never managed to be assertive, to say 'No,' 'Stop,' or 'This isn't what I want.' For a long time, I felt a bitter taste in my mouth. I didn't think I could stop the patterns I was creating in my relationships and my way of being. I also thought others knew better than I did.

So I listened, and did as I was told.

It wasn't right for me, but I have forgiven myself. I am no longer reproducing this pattern, and I invite you to do the same. Others don't know you because you don't show yourself as you really are. They don't understand you because you don't share your frame of reference. I understand what you are feeling right now, so much.

The taste of freedom is such a beautiful gift from life. So, free yourself; do it for yourself and for me. Your bonds are in your mind. You have the potential to break your bonds and create everything you want in your likeness. When flowers come to you, through their perfume, an image or symbol, it will be a sign of my presence and support to help you persevere. You can do it.

SOURCE

YOUR SOUL

You may be having trouble taking a step back and understanding your life path. You are having difficulty finding your place, and you're feeling out of sorts wherever you are. You may be having trouble feeling fulfilled, especially in your work. You also doubt your spiritual abilities and skills. You often question everything, feeling like you're always coming back to square one. This can make you feel exhausted.

Today, connect to your crown chakra and become aware of your karmic line. The point isn't to look for a place you might fit in, but to find ideas so you may discover yourself in a new way. All the signs are before you, but you don't see them because you aren't looking in the right direction.

Look up, and everything will seem much clearer. By becoming aware of your source, you'll become aware of your life path. You will feel well and fulfilled, and you will create your cosy cocoon. While the novelty and unknown will be there, you'll feel safe.

YOUR SPIRIT GUIDES

There is a contradiction in your energy. Part of your energy is blocked in wrong beliefs and negative thoughts. You are centred on what you don't feel capable of, more than on your possibilities. The pace of synchronicities is blocked. Everything is on hold.

You don't have to wait patiently; become aware of this contradiction. It is not negative, but holds a positive warning. This contradiction lets you become aware that you're not fully connected to the energy of confidence.

We also invite you to connect to the law of attraction to create everything you visualise. Speak positively, in the present, and believe in yourself. The more you believe in yourself, the more you will create the paths of potential, move forward serenely, and create new harmony in your thoughts.

THE ENTITY

You may feel like you can't perceive my presence. You may feel like I'm not here, or like you have no 'gift'. Remember, gifts do not exist.

While our relationship has changed, our bond of love is still here. My life helped me understand many things; all the energies I felt helped me to evolve greatly inside. I don't need help, or need to rise up. I am at my source; I am in unconditional love.

From where I am, I have decided to protect you. I am one of your protective angels. I am here as long as you need me. I ask for nothing in return. Deep inside, you know this is my way of asking for your forgiveness and proving my love to you. I am here, guiding you towards yourself, so you may find new inner harmony. I help you to raise your head, because I want you to look at the sun and stop stumbling in the rain.

When you think of me, of us, the word 'falling' may come into your thoughts. Falling is no longer on the cards. We are now on a path of love, stretching on two different planes.

32

YOU

YOUR SOUL

You think you don't know. You think you don't see. You think you are not. You think you cannot.

This is not so.

You're an extraordinary being because you're a spiritual soul in a corporeal experience. You have great inner beauty and wisdom.

Reconnect to yourself. Take a moment to look at yourself in the mirror, and love what you see. Your mistakes, your successes, your wrong paths and your choices. Love your imperfection. You are perfect just the way you are. Look at yourself, and love yourself.

YOUR SPIRIT GUIDES

Everything is inside you. You think you need us, but this is not so. You have all the messages and inner strength you need. You are capable of everything, of moving forward how you would like. Don't look for answers or support outside of yourself. Don't think we know better than you.

We invite you to take a moment; listen to yourself and have confidence in yourself. You can move forward however you would like. You can create what matters to you. Everything is right. Don't let yourself be slowed down by others' frames of reference, or be negatively influenced by outer things. Have confidence in yourself, and be daring.

It's all there. Inside you. And it's beautiful and wonderful.

THE ENTITY

You think you're talking to me, but it's not me. You're communicating with your soul. But today, you need to communicate with me. You expect too much from what is outside of yourself. You lack faith in yourself.

I don't communicate with you to punish you. It's just that, for now, you don't need it. So, I remain silent and let you communicate with yourself. You need to find yourself again. You need to know yourself again.

You have evolved a lot recently, but you don't realise it, so you look for outside support and something to lean on.

Yet, you have many answers inside yourself. Listen to yourself. Understand the messages you hear like an inner conversation. You're talking with a wonderful and splendid person – yourself. This is what you need.

When the time comes, we'll be able to talk together.

SOUL CONNECTION
CARDS' MESSAGES

MESSAGE OF WARNING

This card is here to help you connect to your psychic abilities. Take a moment to visualise the card.

You are invited to receive a message of warning from your soul, your spirit guides or an entity.

Write down what you feel. Look at the card for as long as you need. You are invited to see a message on your own, beyond the card's description. Be confident in yourself.

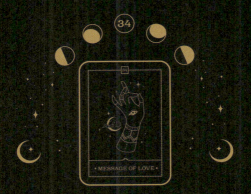

MESSAGE OF LOVE

This card is here to help you connect to your psychic abilities. Take a moment to visualise the card.

You are invited to receive a message of love from your soul, your spirit guides or an entity.

Write down what you feel. Look at the card for as long as you need. You are invited to see a message on your own, beyond the card's description. Be confident in yourself.

MESSAGE OF PEACE

This card is here to help you connect to your psychic abilities. Take a moment to visualise the card.

You are invited to receive a message of peace from your soul, your spirit guides or an entity.

Write down what you feel. Look at the card for as long as you need. You are invited to see a message on your own, beyond the card's description. Be confident in yourself.

MESSAGE OF GUIDANCE

This card is here to help you connect to your psychic abilities. Take a moment to visualise the card.

You are invited to receive a message of guidance from your soul, your spirit guides or an entity.

Write down what you feel. Look at the card for as long as you need. You are invited to see a message on your own, beyond the card's description. Be confident in yourself.

KARMIC MESSAGE

This card is here to help you connect to your psychic abilities. Take a moment to visualise the card.

You are invited to receive a karmic message from your soul, your spirit guides or an entity.

Write down what you feel. Look at the card for as long as you need. You are invited to see a message on your own, beyond the card's description. Be confident in yourself.

MESSAGE OF FREEDOM

This card is here to help you connect to your psychic abilities. Take a moment to visualise the card.

You are invited to receive a message of freedom from your soul, your spirit guides or an entity.

Write down what you feel. Look at the card for as long as you need. You are invited to see a message on your own, beyond the card's description. Be confident in yourself.

FREE MESSAGE

This card is here to help you connect to your psychic abilities. Take a moment to visualise the card.

You are invited to receive a free message from your soul, your spirit guides or an entity.

Write down what you feel. Look at the card for as long as you need. You are invited to see a message on your own, beyond the card's description. Be confident in yourself.

MESSAGE OF FORGIVENESS

This card is here to help you connect to your psychic abilities. Take a moment to visualise the card.

You are invited to receive a message of forgiveness from your soul, your spirit guides or an entity.

Write down what you feel. Look at the card for as long as you need. You are invited to see a message on your own, beyond the card's description. Be confident in yourself.

SPIRITUAL MESSAGE

This card is here to help you connect to your psychic abilities. Take a moment to visualise the card.

You are invited to receive a spiritual message from your soul, your spirit guides or an entity.

Write down what you feel. Look at the card for as long as you need. You are invited to see a message on your own, beyond the card's description. Be confident in yourself.

MESSAGE TO PASS ON

This card is here to help you connect to your psychic abilities. Take a moment to visualise the card.

You are invited to receive a message to pass on to your soul, your spirit guides or an entity.

Write down what you feel. Look at the card for as long as you need. You are invited to see a message on your own, beyond the card's description. Be confident in yourself.

ABOUT THE AUTHOR

Isabelle Cerf is a true lightworker with a degree in Psychology. As an author and speaker, she has been putting her spiritual abilities at the service of others for many years, helping people connect to themselves and their higher purpose. Isabelle looks to create tools enabling people to be empowered in their efforts towards spiritual awakening.

www.lesoraclesdisa.fr
f @lesoraclesdisa
◎ @les_oracles_disa
◎ @isabelle_cerf

ABOUT THE ILLUSTRATOR

Daphna Sebbane is an American illustrator making her life in Austin, Texas. She draws inspiration from Californian culture, the occult and mysticism.

www.daphnasebbane.com
@ @daphnasebbane